Dating Advice

Guide To Enhancing Masculinity, Attracting Desired
Female Partners, Cultivating A Remarkable Relationship,
And Maximising Life's Opportunities

*(Strategies For Achieving Your Desires And Discovering
Your Ideal Partner - Expert Guidance On Online Dating)*

Patrick Higgins

TABLE OF CONTNET

Introduction 1

Ways To Draw In Women 8

Creating A Profile For Online Dating 20

Pique His Interest So He Will Follow You 43

What Women Actually Desire 75

Use Detailed Images To Hypnotize Him. 88

Assess Yourself Thoroughly 102

Introduction

Developing relationships both professionally and personally calls for the same set of abilities. However, if you have been socialized to act more like an android than like a human, you must first rediscover the fundamental abilities that Mother Nature endowed us with.

According to some estimates, mistakes in perception account for 90% of thinking errors. Whether you believe a glance, remark, or action to be flirty on purpose will determine whether you believe that person is flirting with you or not.

Gaining an advantage in the game can be achieved by understanding how various sexes approach flirting. Your chances of getting things going are increased, and your danger of rejection is reduced when you can send out unambiguous indications that could be taken as the start of a flirtation.

Men obsess over the task of crafting the ideal opening phrase for a conversation, while women stress about what to dress. For each sex, such particulars mark the beginning of the flirtation spectrum.

In contrast to the animal realm, where colorful males exhibit courtship displays and dowdy females frequently follow suit, women are supposed to devote more care and attention to their looks. Women typically experience greater pressure to look well, which is why they spend so much time and energy curating and putting together their looks. According to a survey of mostly female office workers, the majority of them took more than three hours to arrange their Christmas party attire, while less than five minutes were spent thinking about conversation starters.

Conversely, men often think that when they open their mouths and say anything flirtatious, they are flirting. They worry so much about what they're going to say because of this. It's also widely accepted that this is the part of your introduction where you run the greatest chance of being rejected. Men can hate this phase the most because they are typically the ones who initiate contact.

Reset your flirtation starting point to the first eye contact to avoid slipping into the trap of obsessing about what you're going to say. Compared to the 'chat-up line' strategy, this interaction is less hazardous and has a greater success rate. You produce more fruitful results and feel better about your flirtatious strategy.

Men

Strangely, attractiveness is rarely listed among the top ten traits for guys. The top of the head replies are consistently the smile, eye contact, bottom, breasts, and legs, which is consistent with the findings of this study. Top responses also include wanting to look and smell well, having long hair and attractive nails, and showing interest in them. It's been said that having wealthy parents and running a brewery are excellent, but not essential, qualities.

Men are obviously quite particular about what they want and don't give a damn about what they don't. When a male first meets a lady, his top three dislikes are having a husband, growing facial hair, and using a phone during a chat.

Instead of worrying about what a man dislikes in a woman, concentrate on what he normally finds attractive in a woman while trying to impress him.

Ladies

Women observed height/stature, a sense of humor, generosity, friendliness, being well-groomed, and, somewhat playfully but consistently, having a sizable wallet when they first met people of the other sex. Bad breath, body odor, haughtiness, cracking jokes, having unnecessary hair, and peering over someone's shoulder rank highest among the dislikes. Telling jokes is sometimes mistaken for entertainment.

It's important to focus on a man's positive traits and minimize his flaws in order to win over a woman.

Studies reveal that males are drawn to one another physiologically. Put another way, they are drawn to shape and color, especially distinct hues that contrast with one another and the outline of the feminine body.

When you wear a subdued black outfit, you blend in with all the other women who have the same wardrobe choice. Although black can hide many transgressions, it's a poor option if it makes you disappear into thin air. Color is like a magnet; however, don't assume you have to walk out dressed like a parrot. Your best bet is to wear colorful clothing to highlight your best qualities or traits.

Women are significantly less particular about the physical characteristics they prefer, with the exception of height. But to be honest, height is a bit of a misnomer; stature is more accurate. It won't do to slouch along like a huge beanpole at six feet tall. A man must project confidence and occupy his area well. A tall man with poor posture is less attractive than a shorter man with excellent posture. So, males, no matter your height, project confidence and stand tall if you want to draw in women.

Not just for flirting but for developing any form of relationship as well, it is crucial to know each other's strengths. These resources work really well with both sexes. The top three resources that are available to all are:

• The way you smile
• Keeping eye contact • Showing real interest in the other individual

By showcasing your shared qualities with everyone you encounter on a social and professional level, you establish a reputation as a person who is genuinely liked and friendly.

Ways To Draw In Women

Do you wish to win a girl over?

Would you like to pique a girl's curiosity at every possible opportunity?

If so, be aware of and abide by the advice given in this section.

First tip: Take Charge of Your Hygiene

These are the top four methods for maintaining hygiene...

To get a beautiful haircut, go to a real barber or hairstylist.

Regular brushing and showering

Develop and take care of a beard or always shave clean. Nowadays, the majority of women find guys with beards more attractive.

Always smell pleasant

The second piece of advice: Wear red.

Do not overdo this.

A woman's perception of red can include sex, attraction, success, or prestige. You will draw attention from ladies if you wear red, even if it's just through your tie or a face hat.

Tip 3: Show You Are Confident.

One of the most significant traits that women look for in men is confidence. The attributes of leadership come second.

Make the first move, like arranging a date or striking up a discussion, to project confidence.

Additionally, when doing so, feel at ease.

Tip 4: Pay Attention to How You Dress

Have you ever heard the saying "dress to be addressed"?

Imagine yourself as a celebrity who is always being photographed to help you focus more on your wardrobe choices.

Would you wear skimpy clothing? Not in my opinion.

Tip 5: Give Your Voice More Resonance

It is a well-established fact that most women are more drawn to guys with deep, rich, resonant voices than to those with the opposite quality.

Practice and use your diaphragm to support your voice to gain resonance.

Furthermore, inhale deeply before speaking.

This will assist you with voice control.

Tip 6: Make an Enduring Impact

This is crucial, of course, if you want the women to think positively of you forever.

The following are the three best methods for achieving this:

Always dress to impress. Here, the focus is always

Create amusing one-liners

Crack jokes

In order to avoid appearing like you are trying too hard, do not attempt to overdo any of this. One step at a time, please.

Tip 7: Get accustomed to wearing a slow smile

According to recent research, women seem to trust males who smile slowly.

Instead of smiling quickly and eagerly, practice smiling calmly.

Tip 8: Feel at Ease with Infants

Playing, chatting, and smiling with infants is a certain method to win a woman over.

When a coworker takes her infant to work, it's one of the simplest methods to locate babies.

Tip 9: Show It Off

Are there any scars on you? Why not show it off? Women often think that a man who has a scar has been in more danger and is thus more manly.

Don't go seeking for one if you don't have one. Incorrect guidance!

Thing 10: Acquire Cooking Skills

According to recent data, women are drawn to guys who are skilled cooks.

Once a date has been decided upon, invite her over to your place so you may prepare dinner for her.

Take my advice if you're just starting out in the kitchen: master one recipe at a time. Make this dish on your next date.

Tip 11: Always Offer Assistance

The three best methods for doing this right now are as follows:

Give back to the community

Take part in the events in your neighborhood.

Give blood

Tip 12: Discover Unique Facts about Her The ideal course of action is to ascertain these. For instance, the destinations she'd love to visit, her ideal meal, and the bands she detests the most.

Knowing these things can help you make a great impression on any woman when you bring them up in conversation at the appropriate moment.

Chapter 2: Gaining Self-Assuredness with Women

Being successful in social situations and possessing confidence are the keys to looking attractive and confident among women. It might be challenging for guys who are more reserved or timid, but developing more self-assurance is essential for approaching and engaging with women. Is there a particular recipe for this? What behavior is expected of you? Furthermore, how can you tell whether something is progressing well? The simplest method to look alluring to women is to project confidence and self-assurance, which is what this chapter will teach you how to do. The truth is that being charming and self-assured without becoming overly self-absorbed requires striking a careful and vital balance.

Consider this careful balancing act as social effectiveness. This is putting in the least amount of work possible to have the greatest possible societal benefit. The most self-assured and handsome people don't seem to need to work very hard; they just naturally and seemingly effortlessly exude beauty. It is obvious when someone tries "too hard," and it is not appealing. Nothing is a faster way to turn off someone you are into and want to date or pursue than to subtly detect when others are desperate, even if you can't exactly figure out why. Effective social beings understand how to make less go farther. You must first comprehend what you shouldn't do in order to comprehend what you should do.

What Turns Women Off: What Should You Avoid Doing?

Too many men never learn what it means to be confident or socially successful in life. They, therefore, find it difficult to connect with girls, go on dates, or make lasting relationships. They can think that in order to make their story more engaging, funny, etc. However, these ideas may cause them to ramble on, failing to seem attractive and drawing ladies in the opposite direction.

The sense that you are undeserving of them: They can tell when you are shy around a pretty female and secretly believe you aren't worthy of their conversation. You must, in all you do, shed this mindset and develop greater self-assurance. You can believe that appearances are everything and that you are doomed if you don't have a specific look. But your attitude and vibe matter more than your physical appearance.

Talking too much: You may try to overcompensate by talking too much to a girl in an effort to impress her, validate your existence, or win their approval when you feel unworthy of her attention. Conversely, you may be impolite or offensive in an attempt to avoid being turned down. It's very off-putting and fully communicates to her that you are nervous. Even if you have everything else going for you, confidence attracts people, regardless of gender. Thus, this could spoil your opportunity. It's time to concentrate on how to pique women's attention, entice them, and eventually go on a date. There are plenty of other methods to turn women off. Try a few different things until you find what works best for your own personality. So, how does a guy learn to become more self-assured?

Developing Your Confidence When Around Women:

The truth is that it's not hard to project confidence around women—something you probably won't believe until you try it and witness for yourself. A lot of guys make the mistake of thinking that they have to learn a lot of rules and behave properly, but in reality, it just comes down to attitude and having the courage to just talk to her, stand your ground, and exist without feeling sorry for yourself.

Thus, the following advice will help you get started in that field:

Develop your walk: Women usually take note of what you're wearing before your walk. After making sure your clothing fits well, you should start paying attention to how you walk and how you hold yourself. Do you always feel like you're in a rush? Strive to go more slowly. A person who exudes confidence is not hurried. This applies to both walking and speaking. Walk as though you know exactly where you're heading and why. Confident people know what they're talking about and where they're walking to.

Establish the Right Amount of Eye Contact: Maintaining eye contact is a strong sign of confidence. You will look fake at worst and insecure at best if you complement her while staring at the floor. Look at her mouth instead of someone's eyes. If you discover that staring into someone's eyes bothers you, it will appear the same to her. If you are going to complement her, make sure it is plausible and grounded in reality. She will roll her eyes if you tell her that she's your ideal lady and that Aphrodite has come to life, but you can probably make her feel good about herself by pointing out that she has nice lips.

Be Confident When Receiving Praise: If a woman tells you how beautiful your eyes or your smile are, accept it with poise and say "thank you." An insecure person will react doubtfully or even give a litany of reasons why the compliment is unworthy, which can be offensive and awkward for the person attempting to be nice. In contrast, a confident person welcomes compliments.

When to Call: We will go into more detail about this in the book when we talk about date etiquette, but in general, you should try to call no later than three days have passed. When a lady gives you her number, you have two days to give it to her; otherwise, you risk looking foolish or afraid if you try to manipulate her. Try convincing yourself that you are on a business call if you are feeling anxious. Consider your date like someone attempting to close a business deal. This can assist in de-stressing you while working.

Don't be scared to leave a voicemail: These days, people don't leave voicemails very often, so make an effort to be different and do this rather than being scared. You want to seem somewhat deep and loud in order to convey confidence. Before making the call, you can try standing up and humming to raise the pitch of your voice to a pleasant and natural level. When you call her, tell her who you are, what time and place you are calling, and why you are calling. Ask her when it would be most convenient for her to get together rather than if she would like to.

Don't Be Negative About Yourself: No matter what you do, try not to be negative when talking about yourself. Rather, concentrate on your good attributes and interests that bring you joy when you talk about them. Talk about your accomplishments and what you want to share with people, not your insecurities and negative opinions about yourself. When someone starts talking negatively about themselves when you first meet them, it raises a number of red flags.

Creating A Profile For Online Dating

The most important factor in your success with online dating is your profile. Whether you're creating a headline or a "about me" section, the goal is to make a statement. You don't want to create a generic profile that girls have seen on several occasions. Knowing the kind of girl you want to date is the first step towards making a unique impression on her. I would advise you to jot down on paper the values, attributes, etc., you are looking for in a female. Jot down as many details as possible, such as if you like gregarious or introverted girls or girls who prefer to plan or are more spontaneous. You may inevitably turn off some girls, but being more explicit about what you want shows that you are not a people-pleaser, needy, or desperate.

Go online and study the males' profiles; most are coming from a selling point, such as, "I drove a Mercedes, I did this, and I have a Ph.D." Where you are saying to a girl, "You are the prize, and I need your validation." You want to be coming from a buying frame. When you are in a buying frame, you already know that you are awesome and have confidence, and you don't need to tell a girl I did this, and I did that. A girl has to work for it to get your approval. If you think about it, you may have met guys who are always bragging about this particular woman they slept with every time they get a chance. They are the ones who usually do not get laid much. If you were getting laid every week or every day, you already have the skills; you wouldn't always be out there talking about girls you've hooked up with every opportunity you get. You might be wondering how she knows I am that cool guy, and the way to do this is to demonstrate. One of the ways is through pictures.

As you know, the picture says thousands of words. Instead of saying you like traveling, upload a cool picture of you with a stunning background while you are traveling. Instead of saying you like music, show her a picture of you playing in the gig.

A counterintuitive tactic that is more effective than you might imagine is to say something like, "I am the guy your mother warned you about," or "I am an avid reader kind of a nerd with commitment issues," to show a girl that you are not desperate and that you are not here to please everyone. This is the second way to stand out from the crowd.

The third approach is to list the things you desire in a female instead of telling her why she should see you and why you are so great. You could write something like, "These are the qualities I look for in a girl," then list those things.

Whoa!

Whoa!

Whoa!

When a great public speaker senses that their audience is about to start using their phone or is not paying attention, they usually say, "All right guys, I'm going to tell you a story." This often results in almost ten percent of the audience paying closer attention. Similarly, tell girls a brief story about yourself when dating online, but don't finish it. Leave them wondering, pique their interest, and make it seem like fun and games. Use language that is attention-grabbing and engaging.

It's important to always put yourself in other people's shoes regarding online dating. You never know what's going through a girl's mind or how many messages she may receive daily. One common trend is that girls are usually aware of what's happening in the celebrity circle and have watched movies at some point. You could use phrases from the movies;

sometimes, I modify them. When you are gaming, girls, it would be a day game or a night game. Note phrases that are working or have worked in the past. Here are some examples:

Ladies, you are not allowed to fight in this war chamber!

I might not be remembered, but I will be remembered for you.

Do you need directions? Well, first, you gotta take this D-tour.

Show that you are a valuable man who doesn't settle down with any girl. You live in a world full of women; you're not desperate and not afraid to be a little picky. Now, I'm going to say something counterintuitive: I have an asshole vibe. You might be wondering why or what that means, and the answer is that you have to do things differently if you want different results. As Einstein once said, "Insanity is doing the same things and expecting different results." The asshole vibe isn't meant to offend people; rather, it simply means that you have boundaries, don't take BS from others, have values, fully express your emotions, are who you are, and don't fake it—you are the real deal. Few men. You don't come across as needy, desperate, or approval-seeking; you know what you want. You also don't prioritize women in your life, as David Deida discusses in his book The Way to Superior Man—a fantastic book you must read! This shows her that you appreciate a lady caring for her health. A female will respect you if you know what you want from her.

Although girls won't confess it, you may have witnessed it in real life—particularly with attractive women who like making fun of other women. I'm not sure how to put it without coming across as a jerk. Still, women who consider themselves attractive but are not particularly attractive are frequently the ones who find this insulting due to insecurity. It may sound strange, but you are doing something incorrectly if you are not receiving the occasional unfavorable answer. If this occurs, you must work on making your profile more controversial and visually striking.

Consider your profile a work in progress; it won't be flawless the first time, especially if you're new to online dating. See what works and then adjust; there is no right or wrong answer. Girls that you are interested in responding favorably and expressing interest even when you only wink at them are signs that your strategy is working.

Work out

1. Write down every trait or idea you want in a female you wish to date for five to ten minutes. As precise as you wish to be.

2. Taking stock of your life. What have you previously received praise for from both foes and strangers, such as your exceptional guitar playing or arithmetic prowess? Usually, this is what makes you strong. In your profile, talk about your areas of strength.

3. Show your female buddy your profile. What is her opinion of it? (You have more work ahead of you if she does not find your profile to be somewhat divisive and disrespectful.)

First Alpha Male Rule: Assume Leadership and Take Charge

Gender Roles: Male and Female

Men like to feel like men.

We love to flaunt our manliness, whether it's by winning a competition, controlling a girl in bed, or getting asked by a lover to open a pickle jar or squash a "scary" large spider. Our goals are to subjugate and defend. We want to feel important and masculine.

This explains the strong attraction that males have to feminine women. This is also the reason that consistently demeaning her partner is the best way for a woman to send him running.

Furthermore, women enjoy feeling feminine just as much as men do.

I'll give you an example to illustrate what I mean:

When you ask a woman, "What do you want to do? You may answer, "I'm happy to do whatever you want," when she asks what movie you want to see, or when you and your companion are choosing which restaurant to eat at, or at any other time. You brush the decision off on her rather than take command of the circumstance and assume the manly role of directing the exchange.

Well, guess what? Ladies detest this. They find it really repulsive as well as offensive. It is not appealing.

You may think she'll love you for it since you're such a "nice guy," and she gets to do what she wants. But it doesn't operate like that. It just gives the impression that you're a weak, insecure man. And never forget that good folks come last.

Women, you see, want to feel like women. They are naturally drawn to and yearn for a man who takes the initiative and leads.

They don't want to be in charge of deciding what to do and where to go. All they want is to follow this self-assured, commanding man around as he goes about his thrilling, daring existence.

Women experience sexiness when they feel feminine. When women are pushed to take on the male role because a guy repeatedly asks, "What do you want to do? They experience annoyance and disinterest.

You act like a man. Allow her to be feminine.

Lesson: Allow her to be a woman by being a man. Lead by example, take command, and let her follow. The feminine follows the masculine. Thus, lead a vibrant, daring life and invite women to accompany you. Don't abdicate your macho obligations to them by asking them the distinctively unsexy, "What do you want to do?"

FROM "HELLO" TO "LAY"

It takes more to be an alpha male than simply never inquire, "What do you want to do?"

It's not enough to only dictate where you go and what you do with ladies; you also need to take the initiative. Everything needs to be under your control.

Observe a lovely woman? Head over and say hello. After a brief conversation, grab her phone number. She ain't going to approach you. Your role is to be the man.

Do you want to arrange a date with a woman you met or have her number? Send her a text to arrange. She won't carry it out for you. Your role is to be the man. (A completely unrelated piece of advice: Instead of calling it a "date," say something like "meet up for coffee" or "grab a drink." That will scare a lot of women away.)

Do you want to start having more intimate moments with women? Grasp her hand. (And, for heaven's sake, don't ask her! Just do it. In the worst-case scenario, she'll jerk her hand away, and you'll have to try again later. But I digress.) Put your arm around her. A loose hair strand should be brushed into place. Women hardly ever start physical contact. Your role is to be the man.

Are you up for a kiss? Maintain eye contact, glance down at her lips, glance back up at her gaze, then slant closer and make a move. As the man, it is your responsibility to start the kiss.

Do you want to tuck her in? "Come have a drink at my place, you've never had a real martini until you've tried my homemade [X]." "I live just around the corner. I have this awesome pool table. Let's go play a round." If you swear not to attempt anything, then you're welcome to visit. After you're in their apartment, just physically advance your approach to having sex. ;) As the man, it is your responsibility to put her to bed.

And so forth.

It's unusual that guys who don't take the initiative or who wait for "just the right moment" to escalate the conversation can win her over.

Chapter 4: How Do You Handle Jealousy and What Role Has It Played in Your Past Relationships?

That famous The Killers song about jealousy and turning snakes into the sea is true, but there's also some truth to it. One of the worst things in the world is jealousy since it causes blindness. It's best to discuss how jealous each of you is as soon as possible.

What causes you to feel envious?

You must first discuss the things that irritate you and the extent to which they can cause jealousy. Examples include ex-partners, friends that talk to your spouse excessively, especially late at night, spending too much time on a pastime to the point where you can't spend time together, certain family members' behavior, etc. Be aware that while you must appreciate these things, you are not required to be jealous of them.

You have to realize that people become envious because of the things that happened to them in the past. Perhaps there was never enough time for each other in a past relationship, or perhaps one or both of you have been betrayed. Somehow, since you care so much about this person and what you have, jealousy is also about trying to keep the connection intact. It's not just about paranoia. Of course, there are instances when envy becomes overwhelming and can become a problem, but you also need to understand that there are steps you can take to avoid it, including providing an answer to the following question.

How Do You Feel About Being Jealous and How Do You Handle It?

When they feel jealous, some people have a tendency to become angry. They may express their annoyance to the other person and, through indirect or direct means, make them aware that they are envious. In essence, they would convey to their partner that they detest what they are doing and that it would be better if they stopped immediately.

In other cases, jealous people usually keep quiet. They will remain silent until the other person becomes concerned and, ideally, reconsiders what he did recently to provoke this kind of response. And if they don't, that can lead to an entirely different kind of issue.

People react to jealousy in different ways, so it makes sense that they would handle it differently as well. Perhaps you want to write about it, post on social media, shout about it, discuss it with your partner, or stalk the other person on social media. The possibilities are endless. The key takeaway is that jealousy has a negative impact on relationships. Therefore, you need to be aware of how the other person behaves when they are feeling it in order to know how to handle it yourself.

Some people have a propensity to be extremely sensitive. However, they occasionally behave haughtily to mask the suffering and insecurity they are feeling on the inside, and they frequently revert to their previous states of inferiority or superiority. They frequently believe that they are the victims, that there is something wrong with them, and that everyone is against them. They are frequently jealous and possessive, and they frequently worry about what their partners will think of them.

If this occurs, or if you are experiencing this, it most likely indicates that you are experiencing vulnerable self-absorption. Yes, you love someone, but you also forget that they are not your property and that you are both on an equal footing in this situation, which can seriously damage relationships.

Regardless of a man's level of confidence, there are moments when he loses self-assurance. It's simple for him to become envious of other men when this occurs.

This is probably nothing new to you. You know, the moments when you try to figure out your partner's password or persuade her to stop texting a certain guy. At times, you might even ask her repeatedly, or you might advise her to stay home rather than go out with friends.

The Green Monster might really take hold of relationships—and not in a good way. Although jealousy may not seem serious at first, if unchecked, it can become quite harmful.

How Much of Your Previous Relationship Was Influenced by Jealousy?

Consider how jealousy affected your previous relationship and reflect on its history. Did you frequently feel envious of the other individuals in your ex's life? Or perhaps it was a matter of time. When you got jealous, how did your ex usually respond? Did you genuinely discuss your issues, or did it get to the point where one or both of you ended the relationship because you were so tired of one other?

How much trust was there in that relationship? What was the experience like? Was your ex genuinely jealous of you, or did you not respect each other enough? What caused your frequent arguments?

By responding to these questions, you will ideally become aware of your mistakes and learn from them so that you won't make the same mistakes twice.

Respect Encourages Respect

It is undoubtedly not the finest combo to be jealous and insensitive. You must learn to treat this individual with respect and give them the impression that you comprehend their jealousy and their perspective if you want them to be in your life forever.

You start to become more watchful of your behavior when you start to become sensitive to the things that irritate your partner. If you continue to act in a way that could harm the other person, even if you don't mean to intentionally damage them, it could be interpreted as a lack of concern for them, which is undoubtedly bad. If you truly care about your spouse, it's best to prevent this from happening because it would somehow give the impression that you have other things to do with your time and that they should probably do the same.

By having early conversations about jealousy, you will teach each other to accept one another's limits and be better equipped to avoid small arguments down the road. Not to mention, it would demonstrate your maturity, which is always a plus.

Consider the positive aspects of your relationship.

In the end, sharing a life with someone is never simple. It's frequently difficult, and occasionally your flaws will win out. There will be difficult days, whether it's your spouse thinking she might not be the perfect fit for you, that she can't seem to be like other people, or you feeling like your tolerance is being tried to the limit.

However, genuine love is able to see past a person's shortcomings, particularly when such shortcomings are not the person's fault. It was not your partner's decision to struggle with jealousy. You have to learn to look past these problems and realize that your partner is not defined by them. You can't hold your partner accountable for their health. None of you wanted this to happen.

Furthermore, people can be incredibly passionate. This implies that they will provide you with the kind of love you will never experience from anyone else since they truly love you with all of their heart and everything they have to give.

It's important for you to keep in mind that both of you need to improve your connection. To ensure that your love is not wasted, it is more important for you both to do everything you can to keep the relationship going.

And you are aware of your abilities?

You can ignore your jealousy and focus on the positive aspects of your partnership. Recall the reasons you selected one another. During difficult times, reflect on the positives. Recall your hobbies and the reasons you are happy about yourself when you are with this individual. Recall your particular reasons for loving this individual. Stop blaming each other—and focus on what you can still do.

Work on it if you want a relationship to last and you are aware of how much can be saved. Even if it might not be the simplest task ever, the effort will undoubtedly be worthwhile.

Points to Bear in Mind:

Dealing with the green-eyed monster is never simple. However, you can be sure that the relationship will succeed if you are aware of what irritates the other person and never purposefully try to provoke them.

What's your dating status? (Chapter 2) Establishing Your Objectives

Setting dating goals is crucial, regardless of whether you're in a committed relationship or are still struggling to find the confidence to ask someone out. By doing this, you'll be able to avoid potential pain, humiliation, needless work, lost time, squandered money, and injuring someone else.

Which dating status do you have?

It's critical to evaluate your present dating circumstances for two reasons. One is that the path of your personal life—and that of your partner—will be determined by the kind of your romantic relationship. The second is that in order to treat the person you are dating with respect, you must be aware of your boundaries.

informal dating

This indicates that you are seeing one other for companionship, light sexual contact, or just to spend quality time together. Insufficient depth is being felt in either emotion to proceed to exclusivity. When dates are irregular, communication is sporadic, you aren't introduced to family or friends, and there are indications that your date is seeing other people, you will know you are in this kind of dating situation.

Short-term dating objectives

It's crucial to avoid becoming overly sensitive in this kind of dating relationship. When you start to feel envious because your date is seeing someone else, it indicates that you are developing feelings for them while your partner has not. When that occurs, be prepared to summon the bravery to sit down and have a meaningful conversation with your date. Declare that you want to go on exclusive dates. Should the other person appear hesitant about it, be prepared to end the relationship since it will only cause you grief in the long run. It is not worthwhile to pursue dating if your objectives are not aligned.

exclusive matchmaking

This indicates that you are not seeing anybody else and that you both share deep romantic love for one another. This typically occurs when you are introduced to personal friends when routines have been established around each other's schedules, when regular and continuous communication occurs, and when intimate physical actions are already being shared.

Does this imply that you've been dating someone already? Because it can be so confusing, this is one of the most frequently asked questions in this kind of relationship status. NO, is the response. At this point, you are not a couple. There must be some form of affirmation between the two of you before you can be considered a couple. This can be expressed verbally, like when you tell each other, "I love you," or it can be discussed openly, like when you announce you are already a couple.

Any kind of intimacy, whether it be verbal or physical, used to be a dead giveaway that two people were a couple and should be seeing each other only. However, being close to one another does not always imply exclusivity in these more liberal times. For this reason, it's critical to communicate. If at all possible, you should be able to verbally clarify that you are ready to start a relationship or that you are already dating exclusively.

Long-term relationship aspiration

If you're in a romantic relationship right now, you should have a clear idea of where you want it to go. This involves making efforts that will assist your relationship in advance, such as introducing your date to family and friends, going out of the country together, synchronizing your job and personal life, and organizing more bonding times together.

Obviously, long-term dating objectives only result in marriage as the ultimate outcome. It's acceptable to take your time getting to know one another even better, though. When they eventually discover a problem they can't work through together, even long-term dating couples find themselves in Splitsville. It is crucial to utilize this unique and delightful dating period to get to know each other's personalities, as well as our own aspirations, ambitions, and future plans.

Pique His Interest So He Will Follow You

If you want your ex back, you must make him chase you. Many women who enjoy studying or reading about men are aware of this.

Well, when you stop and think about it, convincing someone else to ardently seek a romantic relationship with you is not an easy task. However, I intend to change that using the advice given below.

Recall that the less emotional and more rational lady usually wins out in the end when it comes to winning your ex back. I'm not suggesting that being emotional is always a bad thing, but if you're attempting to attract someone's attention, it might definitely backfire.

Avoid being a sentimental texter.

This person double-texts people with extremely sentimental messages like "Are you there?" "why aren't you answering me?"

"ANSWER ME," and "Okay, don't bother talking to me ever again."

I want you to witness this person's terrible appearance. She initially texted to inquire as to whether the other person was present. She grew more and more irate as time passed, and she received no response. Now, the problem with emotional texters is that if your ex thinks you're one, he won't be as likely to chase you because you won't have anything left to enjoy the excitement of the chase with.

The key to getting your ex-boyfriend to pursue you once more is patience, along with a little bit of luck and tactics. There are two rules for this. Both the patience in contact and the patience when there is none.

Calm without making contact: a time when you don't talk to your former partner. Typically lasting thirty days on average. This implies that you don't respond to him if he reaches you and that you are under no circumstances permitted to get in touch with him while he is off the radar.

The no-contact policy is wonderful because of this. It provides you time to collect yourself and not only offers your ex an opportunity to miss you. Naturally, the majority of women who attempt no contact and fall short do so because they lack the patience and/or confidence to convince their ex to pursue them.

Avoid doing the following during the no-contact period: -Spending the day in bed because you're upset.

-Avoid going out and staying at home.

-Intoxicating oneself.

-Announcing your split to everyone.

-Making significant life choices.

- Regularly missing work.

Some food for thought: In this period of no communication, he will most likely attempt to text or phone. It's crucial that you disregard him.

-Mutual friends might tell you that he has been calling you derogatory names, or you might get the impression that he despises you and doesn't want to interact with you. He is simply acting out because he is upset; don't worry about it. In any case, he will undoubtedly alter his mind after 30 days.

Being patient when interacting: The opposite of not communicating with your ex is staying in touch with them. It's the time when you can have conversations with your ex-boyfriend.

As difficult as it was to be patient during the 30-day time without communicating, getting back in touch with your ex after you successfully completed the no-contact phase can be much more difficult.

If you want to be pursued by someone, you should probably utilize quality block texting as your only tactic while texting anybody, not just your ex. A TV show is meant to leave you wanting more with a cliffhanger so that you tune in the next time. This is an example of excellent blocking. Now, just like with TV shows, this also applies to your SMS exchanges with persons you are interested in. I'll explain why in a moment.

But that's not all. Text him again and keep doing this until you've hooked him, about three to five hours after you've interrupted the conversation with a cliffhanger. Can you see what's happening here? The texts are being divided into chunks of quality time that are entirely under your control. When the texts start and end, it is entirely up to me. Still, there are a lot of anomalies associated with that. To apply the QBT approach correctly, a great deal of logical reasoning is required. It can be rather difficult to stop a conversation with your ex if you're already building a solid rapport with them. However, you must use logic to decide when to stop. A certain level of comfort goes into "getting replies," and it can be difficult to know when to end a conversation when emotion is there.

2. What Do You Want to Find?

It's crucial for a lot of people to have wonderful relationships in their lives. If you want this relationship to support you in keeping an upbeat and effective mindset, it needs to be strong and meaningful. This mention of that special someone provides you with consolation when you need it, emotional and intellectual stimulation when you desire it, and the reciprocation of your simple love. Meeting your wants and meeting your partner's needs are both possible in a great relationship.

It is imperative that you use caution in your relationships as a result of this. It's using a long-term approach to prevent you from progressing psychologically. The amount of tension and anger you both carry around may be influenced by the way you communicate with your partner. Your happiness may also be impacted by this. It has been demonstrated that the stronger your relationship, the less probable it is that you will experience depression.

A special someone is necessary in everyone's life. You'll feel prosperous if you create a good friendship. You'll be happier the farther you reach to engage in meaningful engagement with someone. But it should be a healthy kind of connection for you. It's critical to comprehend the goals you have for the relationship. As a result, you should consider what you want out of a relationship.

Pose inquiries such as: Describe your relationship goals in detail.

Do you hope that you and your spouse will be able to do more in a variety of ways?

Would you like to be a part of a relationship where you get along well with others, or do you occasionally think that spending time with good individuals would be preferable?

Would you desire to develop into someone who enjoys growing their social network for both personal and professional purposes, and would you like assistance getting over your shyness?

If any of these apply to you, you should next be sure to identify the reasons behind your desires for those specific aspects of your relationship. Would you like to express that life is more enjoyable? Are you attempting to prevent yourself from experiencing loneliness right now? Is it possible that you would like to increase your own self-assurance?

You can add your own questions to the list, but you should definitely try to figure out the answers to those first before you start adding to it. Your aspirations to have things work out to meet your requirements will be more successful the more overtly you look for what you want from your relationship. You'll know you're in the best possible relationship for you when a lot of these factors work together.

Now it's time to rest and choose what you look for to accomplish within your partnership as well as the causes of yours. All you have to do is pick a specific goal to start with. Next, decide how that will help you to fortify the connection that you desire in your life. You will have a great outcome in your relationship when you think positively.

3. Conversation on First Date

Talking on a first date is crucial because a lot of first impressions are made during this period. These initial impressions are important in determining whether or not to schedule a follow-up appointment. Therefore, the person would need to be seen as a good conversationalist or, at the very least, have the capacity to come up with intriguing topics to discuss in order to ensure that another date is definite rather than probable.

Securing An Additional Date

When trying to strike up a conversation on your first date, there are a few key things to keep in mind. These include practicing, coming up with excellent questions, and being aware of the purpose of the date. It wouldn't be hard to get off to a great start if the person had all of this organized neatly in their mind.

In order to keep the discussion going back and forth, the individual completing the practice segment will need to come up with some excellent questions that are appropriate for the situation or date and have intriguing answers. One can become proficient at ensuring that the topic being discussed retains the level of fluidity and flow from the conversation by practicing with friends and family.

The evident understanding of the date's purpose—that is, to quickly get another date—will then be your next step to master. In order to do this, the individual must make the other person's experience exciting enough to make a second date seem straightforward. Ensuring a nice time might be the top focus because people who enjoy their first dates might desire to go on another one. Another issue is coming across as confident while starting the conversation. The degree of arrogance displayed can make it possible for someone else to be impressed with the person and want to go on a second date.

Incredible Scientific Theories About Dating

Let's now talk about the several scientific theories that most guys enjoy discussing when it comes to attracting women to date. Numerous dating specialists have authored dating books and pick-up guides, and if you enjoy reading them, you'll always find some bizarre scientific theories applied to dating. While the majority of their theories are founded on lies, some of them are genuinely true. Yes, they frequently boast about a scientific hypothesis for which there is no solid evidence, and we frequently fall for their falsehoods without fail.

You will learn the appropriate strategies in this chapter to ensure that your dating endeavors are successful. Naturally, this chapter will also give you some knowledge about the hypotheses put forth by other specialists, as well as the rationale behind some of them being wholly unhelpful.

As already stated in the chapter before, the peacocking notion is untrue. This is because the majority of males dress ostentatiously when they visit bars and discos. Because of this, there will always be someone else wearing more costly and vibrantly colored apparel than you, even if you dress to impress.

Let's now disprove a few of the scientific beliefs you frequently come across on the internet. Using magic words to seduce someone is one of them. Many websites provide you with expert guidance based on NLP or convincing statements that subtly influence your target. In actuality, it is completely foolish to hypnotize someone to get them to perform what you desire. You will never win her heart, no matter how hard you attempt to win her over with some enchanted words. This is because hypnosis is an illusion. It's a cheap technique used in parlors to extort money from people.

The next thing you'll hear a lot about online are the miracle drugs and sprays that can make you a better player. The sprays you find online are frequently based on pheromones, which are chemicals that signal to women and raise their desire. Actually, pheromones that you purchase online are sometimes created by mixing water and scent. Some even come from the testicles of baboons and lions. The magic pills are either dangerously blended drugs or sugar pills, both of which are prohibited in many nations.

The negation hypothesis is the last one. According to this notion, your chances of getting beyond a woman's defenses and into her life increase the more insults or unfavorable comments you make. The negative things you say about women include things like how typical they seem, how simple their clothes are, how small they are, how big their bodies are, or how talkative they are. This theory can really harm your chances, in addition to being offensive.

What, therefore, makes the negation hypothesis false? The emotional nature of most women is the cause. When you give them negative comments, they often feel horrible and quickly become offended. They might spill their drink all over your face instead of focusing on you. They might even get you kicked out of the club by calling the bouncers inside. For this reason, it is never a good idea to approach women using the negation theory.

How to Raise Your Game Right Away

Naturally, not every dating-related theory you hear is untrue. Some are based on years of research by university professors and their students, as well as actual scientific data. You can increase your game and get a girlfriend at the same time by adhering to their theories.

The beer goggles theory is one of these. According to this hypothesis, women choose men depending on their time. This theory was verified by scientific study. The study found that women are generally less fussy in the late hours of the night than they are during happy hour. The explanation is that most women hook up in the early hours of the night out of desperation. Therefore, if you start looking for a girl at night, your odds of finding someone to hook up with are better.

Another notion is centered on the way women dress in relation to when they ovulate. Most women tend to exhibit more skin if they are available or if they are ovulating. Therefore, if you try to pick up ladies based on their wardrobe, the odds of finding the appropriate woman for you will be significantly better. You will also be able to hook up with more women.

Another thing that you need to learn about women is the element of similarities. This factor is based on how many things you share in common with the ladies whom you date. For instance, if you enjoy the same brand of cake, or you both love to go to the park, or you like the same television shows or music, the more similarities that you have with a lady, the better the possibilities of you hooking up with her and eventually being her partner. So, if you want to have a girlfriend who will stay with you for a long time, find one that enjoys your music and style.

The Issue with Courtship

The key to winning at dating is the guts to approach a woman and ask her out. Do you have what it takes to successfully meet and attract the woman of your dreams? When you see her, will you be brave enough to introduce yourself? Or will someone else get her, and he ends up with her instead of you, even though you know deep down that he probably doesn't deserve a lady like her?

One question summarizes the entire exhilarating dating experience: will it be you or someone else? You should never assume that it is any more complicated than that. It's not. If you do not have the necessary tools and the proper mindset needed to make your darkest desires come true with the woman of your dreams, then you are going to accept an eternity of absolute frustration or of watching all the actions happen to someone lucky or more skillful than you.

The worst part of this is that, even how annoying it is to see less attractive men hook up with the most attractive women, many men still do nothing to change the pattern or improve their chances. Men who experience this tragedy end up settling for women who don't even suit their tastes, leading to an unfulfilled life if they find a partner.

Your Self-Asked "Scary" Questions

You may wonder, then, why this occurs. This occurs due to these men's failure to recognize and execute the first, most crucial, and vital action they ought to have taken. That is to say, they were never brave enough to overcome their dread of approaching elegant, well-bred women.

Therefore, ask yourself this before learning more about dating: how much do you want to date the ideal woman? Furthermore, are you really prepared to fulfill your dreams at last?

You should start by asking yourself the inquiries that you may have answered repeatedly in your head, such as the following:

Do you find it impossible to come up with something to talk about with a woman you like when you finally work up the nerve to approach her?

Even though it could seem that you are doing nothing wrong or that you are doing everything correctly, are you sick and tired of experiencing rejection?

Do you want to meet the woman of your dreams without putting in a lot of work, but you're not sure where to start looking? Indeed, you know that a setting like a pricey, dark, and boisterous pub is not the place to find that kind of woman.

At any time in your life, have you had overwhelming worry about meeting ladies because the more successful and manly you have gotten, the more nervous you get?

Do you feel annoyed by the fact that you don't know when to start looking for a lady or where to go to meet any woman at all, even if you know deep down that you deserve to meet a great and attractive woman?

Have you ever sat in bed and wondered how in the world the fear and terror associated with meeting women came to be?

Or, if you make it to that point at all, do you lie in bed at night confident that you will ace your first date with a stunning woman?

Do you want a high-quality lady instead of just a string of one-night encounters, but you don't want to utilize pickup artists' chat-up lines or dirty techniques to acquire what you want?

If not all of the questions on this list, then it's nearly a given that many of you have already asked yourselves at least one. Furthermore, you are all too familiar with the events that follow once you set eyes on the woman of your dreams: She embodies all your desires in a woman: she is stunning, ladylike, and unquestionably your type.

She is exquisite in every manner imaginable, as though God created her only for you. And there she is, by herself, standing just in front of you. She has such a powerful sex appeal that it catches your attention and makes you question what on Earth you might use to introduce her.

It is imperative that you meet her; you know that much. Your instincts are telling you to have the guts to approach her because you are so desperate to meet her that it feels as though your life depends on it. You are aware that you must act immediately or that you must take advantage of the chance before it passes.

This is the point at which everything breaks down. You will undoubtedly fall short of making that crucial initial impression if you are like most males in the world.

You don't reveal your true self to the woman who has captured your attention. Something about this scenario is blatantly incorrect. But don't worry—you're not the only one who feels this way.

Many males have experienced what you have, and many more are likely experiencing it at this very moment. The awful thing about this is that if you don't take proactive measures to address it, it can get worse. This is where this book is helpful.

A significant portion of guys who experience and live with this phobia will never, ever be able to have the courage to approach and confidently introduce themselves to women they have never met before.

Section Three

Cats Are Indifferent to Your Opinion

One of the many fascinating traits of the cat is its attitude. They stroll around as though they are successors to an unseen throne; heads held high and noses in the air. What you think is irrelevant to cats. They follow their own desires rather than your wishes. This is why we enjoy cats. We think it humorous and admirable.

Cats don't experience guilt for their actions or inactions. They don't care that they gained a few pounds or that they aren't the most attractive cat on the street. Cats are naturally self-assured. a self-assurance that demands, "Where's my dinner, screw all of you?" A cat can act like the world's greatest gift, even if it has crap smeared into its fur and litter hanging off its ass. Cats don't feel the slightest bit of shame about what they accomplish during the day. Furthermore, why not? Why should people expend time and effort trying to feel differently?

Imagine a world where women did the same.

Cats are the epitome of the "zero fucks given" mentality and complete self-assurance that a woman needs to possess in order to succeed in life and in love. Hear me out before you believe this is just another chapter in a book on dating tips and confidence. There is much more at stake here than confidence. That has to do with reprogramming.

If you've ever read a dating guidebook, you are well aware of the importance of confidence. Again, we've heard it all before. Blah, blah, blah have self-assurance. Well, easier said than done. For this reason, reading it and putting it into practice are two wholly different things. This explains why, even after reading a thousand books or advice columns, we are unable to achieve true confidence.

If you're one of the many women who suffer in this area, remember that you're not alone. Even the most self-assured women occasionally experience low self-esteem and self-doubt. That's because it's deliberate to make women feel inferior to men. We were taken advantage of by this tool, and we fell for it head over heels. That's why the cat wisdom of "not giving a fuck" will be essential to your life as a woman, regardless of where you stand on the spectrum of self-esteem. However, if you've tried and failed to build confidence and you know that it's harming your ability to date, succeed with men, and possibly even succeed in life—this chapter will completely shift your perspective.

The Subliminal Process

As you may have heard, confidence plays a crucial role in drawing the other sex. This is entirely accurate. The issue lies in the fact that no book can solve a woman's lack of confidence until we address the fundamental issues preventing us from achieving that confidence. We are going to go down the rabbit hole, so be ready.

First and foremost, we must acknowledge that women have been socialized to think negatively and experience tension, worry, and guilt for hundreds, if not thousands, of years.

To put it another way, we've been raised to care way too much about what other people think and to compromise to the point that it interferes with our own internal conversations. Our default setting has been to give up inner serenity in order to please other people.

For others, these deeply rooted negative thought patterns develop into more serious issues, including melancholy, anxiety, self-doubt, low self-esteem, and indecision.

The primary issue is that our decisions and behaviors are influenced by these ideas and feelings.

This mental training is intended to MANipulate our actions. It forces us to conform, encourages obedience, and keeps us in check. It promotes...submission.

Since it has persisted for so long, most of us aren't even aware of how its slimy tentacles are beginning to infiltrate our daily thoughts and deeds. These thought patterns and reflexive reactions are ingrained in the psyche of every woman on the planet because they are so intricately woven into the fabric of our lives. True, some women are far more adept than others at spotting it and turning it down, but we're all vulnerable.

This chapter will assist you in realizing this, enabling you to permanently remove the programming and unleash an unadulterated, natural confidence that will make you utterly alluring to men. More importantly, you will be able to unleash your inner power—the divine feminine power that has been purposefully suppressed for centuries by patriarchal programming—by discovering this true confidence. It is true that we have come a long way toward equality, but we still haven't fully recovered from the male-driven subconscious programming that initially kept us in check and controlled us. Since identifying the issue is half the battle, let's start by going over it in detail. We can proceed to remove the problem once we can see it clearly.

MANipulations

Here are a few instances of programming that subtly influences women's attitudes and behavior. The following list aims to be a collection of examples and definitions rather than a list of generalizations. I understand that not all women and men are functioning in these ways, but in order to make a point, it's critical to present a clear picture of these control mechanisms. Prior to going over this list, I would also like to point out that, regrettably, we women also inflict a lot of this negative programming on one another; it has become such a commonplace behavior. As you read this, I want you to observe that although men and women rarely do these things to one another, they do them to women and other women.)

Accusations of guilt: Controlling someone by inducing guilt, making someone feel bad in hopes that it will change their course of action. Humiliating or demeaning someone in an effort to influence their attitudes, convictions, or behavior. It is also defined as a guilt trip. Causing one to feel responsible or guilty, especially when it is not warranted a conviction that one's approval is contingent upon one's compliance with one's demands.

The following is a very short list of the things that women have been socialized to feel bad about. The list goes on and on and on until you feel like screaming! Some examples of these include not being married by a certain age, having too many children, not having children, being fat or thin, being sexy or not sexy, being a pushover or too aggressive, aging, your religious beliefs, your sex drive or lack thereof, your cooking or cleaning skills, and more!

Double Standards: A rule, principle, or expectation that is unfairly applied in different ways based solely on the sex of the person. Pay disparities between men and women are among the instances. Men who have several sexual partners are rewarded, while women are viewed as slutty. While women are expected to be good mothers and devoted wives, men are praised for being good fathers and faithful husbands. Men are expected to work full-time and take care of the home minimally, while women are expected to work full-time and raise children and maintain the home. Also referred to as uneven domestic workloads. Men who are single are praised for being "happy and carefree bachelors," but women who are single are told they "can't keep a man."

Poor Self-Worth and Self-Esteem: Low self-esteem and low self-worth are perhaps the most powerful tools in the oppression of women's lives because they cause women to feel horrible about their identities, appearances, behaviors, and other aspects of themselves. Because of their conditioning, women are expected to have a delicate sense of self that is easily hurt by the opinions of others. Healthy self-esteemed women are made to feel ashamed of being at ease in their own flesh by being called bitches, haughty, or conceited. Women who show confidence in spite of blatant flaws are subjected to additional mockery, shame, and treatment as though they are completely insane for rejecting and disobeying social criticism. The idea that it's improper for women to feel good about themselves, particularly if they have flaws, is reinforced by this kind of shame. The repressed and imbalanced mindsets that follow are also supported by the deeply rooted and widespread low self-esteem and low self-worth that are imposed on women:

Pressure to Uphold Ideal Physical Form: valuing a woman primarily based on how she looks. This shames people who do not fit in with society's current definitions of sexiness and places an absurd amount of pressure on women and girls to maintain physical perfection. For instance, you couldn't be curvaceous enough thirty years ago, and you can't be skinny enough now. The styles change, but the message is consistent: you're not enough as you are. Being made fun of and disgusted by naturally occurring physical characteristics like cellulite, stretch marks, loose skin, sagging or small breasts, etc. Feelings of guilt, shame, and internal turmoil over things over which we have no control are brought on by all of this pressure to achieve physical perfection. For certain women and girls, this results in a mental prison of self-loathing.

What Women Actually Desire

How many happy, fulfilling partnerships do you observe in the world?

Divorce occurs in 40% of marriages in the UK. It's far worse in the US. Fifty percent of marriages terminate with death.

The worst part is that these startling figures don't even account for the unhealthy partnerships maintained by couples who choose to stay together "for the kids" or just because they are unable to pay for a divorce.

Why are partnerships so often unsatisfactory and failing?

For two factors.

First, there aren't enough actual males in the world. Husbands and fathers aren't "showing up." They're not accepting accountability.

As a result, the cycle also affects their generation as their children grow up without understanding what it takes to be in a fulfilling relationship.

Now, this reason should not cause you any trouble if you completed all of the activities in Part I of this book. You're heading toward true manhood, and as long as you don't stray from the path, everything will work out.

It's the second thing you should be concerned about right now.

Men don't understand what women want, which is the second reason that so many relationships fail.

What ARE the desires of women?

You're in a little bit of danger if all you know about women comes from the mass media, what women SAY they want, or what your friends say about them.

First things first:

Never Heed Women's Advice Regarding Women

Have you ever encountered something like this before?

Despite her stated desire for a "kind, loyal, hardworking gentleman," the lady she ends up with is an abusive cheater.

Or a woman offers you her number but doesn't get back to you.

Or you stop paying attention to a woman who acts coldly toward you, only to get angry texts asking why you're ignoring her.

If you haven't already, take up this lesson: Women NEVER express their desires. This isn't always done purposefully, but at least they can never say it honestly and truthfully.

How many times, I ask you, have you heard a woman declare she wants a kind gentleman who will wine and dine her, only to have the exact opposite happen?

Women often have a clear notion of what they think they want, but what truly attracts them may be quite different.

Women may urge you in the way they want you to go, as you will discover later in this book. However, never heed their dating advice.

Are All Women Liemers?

Being straightforward, "keeping it 100," and maintaining your word are all traits associated with men.

Women adhere to distinct regulations. Feelings are more trustworthy than facts with women.

That's not to imply they don't communicate rationally, though. They can, and they frequently do when they're feeling good.

However, when they're angry or passionate, they ignore the facts and simply believe their own emotions.

Here's an illustration. I once informed my ex-girlfriend that I was going to fetch Chinese food for us to eat.

"No, I don't like Chinese food," she informed me.

I then took her hand and spun her around, and we kind of did this ridiculous, awkward dance that made her laugh.

We took a moment to gather our thoughts before I suggested we grab some sweet and sour prawn balls.

As expected, she responded, "Sure!"

We also enjoyed some quite tasty prawn balls.

When she claimed she didn't enjoy Chinese food, was she lying to me?

Naturally, no. At that precise moment, she was simply acting on her feelings or her "truth." That's women for you; it's subjective rather than objective.

Now for the fundamental guideline: Don't take anything, she says seriously unless it comes from the heart unless she is bursting with love. Rather, trust your own judgment and go with your instincts.

And speaking of trusting your instincts.

Never Take Advice on Dating from Friends

It's also not a good idea to ask your pals for dating guidance.

Why not?

Since they will advise you based on their perceptions of what is best for you.

They won't always tell you what functions.

Thus, generally speaking, you should only seek advice from friends whose relationships you aspire to be similar to. If not, appreciate their counsel, but go with your instincts.

What Do Women Actually Want, Then?

What's the solution to our urgent inquiry now that you know where NOT to obtain dating advice from? What are women's true desires?

Once more, you go to science for a trustworthy response.

Psychology has discovered over the past 100 years or more that women have three essential wants in life: the need to feel monetarily supplied, the need to feel psychologically safe, and the need to feel physically protected.

The "basic math" of making a lady happy for the rest of her life is this. If you can make her feel all three, she will be permanently in love with you; if you can only make her feel one, she will just see you as one of her many possibilities, and probably not the greatest one.

Let's examine each essential need in more detail, one at a time.

First need for women: a sense of psychological security

A woman needs mental tranquility. She must know that she can fully rely on you. It is only at that point that she will be able to let go of her need to maintain appearances, protect her reputation, and be completely herself.

Put differently, she needs a strong, focused, and charismatic guy to guide her—someone whose passions are completely under his control.

Don't get me wrong, though. I support gender parity in academia and the business sector.

However, I oppose FORCED equality, like that promoted by third-wave feminism and the labeling of masculinity as "toxic."

In fact, one could argue that "progressive" ideals like these are the reason why half of marriages nowadays end in divorce.

The polarity between male and feminine energy is eliminated by these new concepts, and when you subvert sexual attraction, everything else falls apart like a set of dominoes.

What, then, is a man to do?

Easy: Act like a man. And these are a few tried-and-true methods for developing your masculinity:

Unless you are attending a funeral, never display weakness. If you must vent, save it for your male pals rather than your partner.

Never implore or grovel. Never give up control of your destiny to a woman. Adhere to your core beliefs and pursue your life's purpose. She follows you if she truly loves you.

Adhere to the maxim "My way or the highway." You SHOULD have the courage to leave a lady who tries to control you, even if you should never abdicate your obligations.

Chapter 1: The Greatest Locations to Meet New People

Almost anywhere is a good place to meet new people. On the other hand, meeting new people is typically easier in some locations. That's what this chapter will address initially. So, where are the best places to meet new people?

In addition to being teeming with people from all walks of life, parks provide a perfect environment for mingling with strangers. They also provide a calm setting that fosters an atmosphere that is ideal for striking up and continuing discussions. If you want to meet new people, parks should be at the top of your list of locations to visit.

Celebrations

Festivals, be they musical, cultural, or religious, offer others you might not have encountered otherwise.

Similar to parks, festivals have an upbeat vibe that makes it appropriate to approach strangers and strike up a discussion. Most festival-goers are generally upbeat, which makes it simple to connect with someone and strike up a conversation. Don't ignore the neighborhood celebration or write it off as being too busy or inappropriate as a location to meet new people.

Other locations where you can meet new individuals and possibly even your soul mate are fitness and health clubs with saunas, yoga studios, aerobic centers, gymnasiums, etc.

sporting occasions like Wimbledon Parties and the Super Bowl

Volunteering endeavors

You will meet at least one person in any of these locations that you will like and want to talk to. When you come across someone like that, you have to be careful how you approach them.

Let's get into more detail about how to do that to increase your likelihood of finding the right partner:

How to Make the Correct Approach to New People

Here's what to do if you see someone you'd like to talk to and approach while in any of the aforementioned locations—or anyplace else, for that matter—:

#: Boost your own confidence

It's just not the right fit; there is no "rejection." There's a reason you are pulled to that someone. It's possible that this is because our meetings are prearranged. You will never know until you step outside of your comfort zone, take the risk, and find out for yourself, even if preordination isn't the reason you're drawn to a particular man or woman—which is okay, too.

Before approaching a stranger, it's normal and acceptable to feel anxious. Keep in mind that the more anxious you are, the more important you think that person is, and the less likely it is that you will approach them.

Play to your strongest traits that make you a desirable person once you've caught their attention. Keep your feelings of inferiority at bay. Rather, affirm yourself by saying, "I am perfect for this person." Someone just like myself has been sought after by this person.

It is easy to feel secure enough to approach someone when you have such an attitude. Now that we are discussing how to make your move:

#, Initiate a dialogue

Approach the individual with the intention of doing the task that most people find most difficult: having a conversation with someone you like. There's something you should know before we discuss how to do that correctly.

Speaking with a complete stranger or someone you don't know well demonstrates your bravery and confidence; conversing with someone you want to attract.

Acknowledge and understand that having vulnerability is a charming quality in a person. You are usually more genuine and appealing than someone who employs staged moves when you act normally around the individual you wish to impress.

Make sure you keep eye contact and give them a nice smile before approaching someone you want to talk to. Although it's not always natural, if you're a woman, that portion is crucial. According to experts, the majority of men won't approach a woman unless she sends them this kind of indication.

If you are a man, you should be aware that a woman is more inclined to approach you or be more "inviting" if you can initially connect with her energy through her eyes.

You will feel a little more confident to approach the person you want to chat with and keep making polite eye contact and smiling. You should still speak up even if you are not feeling confident for any reason.

The hardest thing about striking up a conversation with a stranger is deciding what to say. You can strike up a conversation in a million different ways, so it doesn't have to be. Saying "Hello" while wearing a smile is the simplest method to strike up a conversation. How's it going, and how are you?

Give the other person an opportunity to react once you've said this, then carry on the conversation. Don't do anything that you wouldn't normally do with a buddy of the other sex, such as running into her or stumbling over him. Simply be who you are.

Express your interest in the person, and keep in mind that it's okay to like someone. As previously stated, displaying vulnerability is a desirable quality when courting.

Use Detailed Images To Hypnotize Him.

You may have noticed that many cutesy texts have eye-catching images emphasizing the phrase "How much I love you." Here's our second secret: using powerful imagery is the best method to get and hold his attention (even if it's a reply text). Any visual imagery you can think of would help, as men are visual creatures.

Now, remember that when we discuss visuals, we mean vibrant images like those found in paintings or movies. But while we're messaging each other, you can also use vivid concepts from other senses, like sound, touch, smell, taste, etc.

These texts of "allure" are quite mesmerizing. He must see the pictures to comprehend what you're saying. He visualizes the scene in his head. He experiences the image viscerally, or at least the feelings evoked by the striking sight. He will quickly feel another hypnotic suggestion if you describe anything else, like a cold breeze or a whisper in his ear—all thanks to writing on a screen!

Strong visual imagery is one of the best ways to flirt with your guy, as you may have guessed by now. Therefore, consider telling stories with strong images rather than merely talking about your sentiments when you see strong visuals. Not even an explanation of what you're doing is necessary.

Simply narrate brief stories and cutaways from real events, even the unremarkable details of daily existence. However, make sure the sentence contains a powerful visual cue that evokes his physical yearning for you.

You're pushing him to picture it if you say something like, "Sorry for the late response...was taking a long shower." Or even a seemingly innocuous statement like, "I had to put clothes on," could be a subtle but useful method of stimulating his mind and eyes.

He's going to think of you in that circumstance, with those powerful images, every time from now on. This explains the potency of sexual imagery, particularly for those who have never experienced sex or have only had it once. You genuinely intensify the suspense and expectation for your next encounter. Now, all those pictures are circling around his head, stoking his thoughts about you.

That's the reason I always believe that fewer texts are better and more valuable. Give them some thought and take your time. Send him a unique text message that will make him feel and see amazing things. Because of this, he will always be astounded by your texts. Not at all dull!

ILLUSTRATIONS

"Every time you call me on the phone, I still get butterflies in my stomach!"

"There are times when I dream that we're at the beach, having a lovely conversation under the bright sun."

Imagine that I'm hugging you tightly. A warm cuddle with a huge sweater. That will help you stay warm on this chilly evening.

When you gaze at me, sometimes your eyes seem to be filled with moonlight. Indeed, even via webcam.

"I need a bubble bath badly. All you need is a glass of wine and a lengthy, soothing bath. Does that not sound fantastic?

Section 7: The Dog Park

When you have a dog, this is the greatest place for you to approach women. Or even for them to approach you. Women just can't help themselves when it comes to a lovely puppy. In the world of pick-up, dogs are your best friend and support system, so what they say about them being a man's best friend is true. You just need to take your dog for walks, give it some playtime, and give it some attention.

If you're lucky, a lovely woman will say something about your puppy or smile at you while you play. Seize the moment to play with your dog with her as well, or even just tell her a little bit about it. A sweet method to ask her out is to suggest, after a few minutes of conversing, that your dog and her dog go on a play date to get to know one other better.

You can use this opportunity to interact with women instead of waiting for them to approach you and beg to play or pet your dog. When you tell a woman that her dog is cute, she usually feels flattered and invites you to play with it. In a perfect world, your dog would approach the most attractive girl's dog, and they would play or trade butt sniffs, but in real life, you'll mostly have to rely on your own social skills. Luckily, not much is needed in this case; you may let your dog's cuteness complement yours until you're confident enough to approach the girl for her phone number.

Chapter 8: The Shore

Bronze-buffed surfers and other macho characters can be fierce competitors on the beach, so it's not for the weak of heart. Beautiful women are also there, showing off their own bikini-clad, tanned bodies while having fun in the surf. Girls can be found sunning alone, with friends, or both here.

Even if you are there with friends, it is still preferable to approach them alone if they are alone. Friends are useless in this situation since approaching a woman with a bunch of guys would only intimidate her. You can make comments about what she's reading, if it's a book or magazine, or you can just sit down next to her and smile.

The trick is to focus exclusively on her face and try your best not to glance at her body. Simply say hello, remark on how lovely the weather is, inquire as to whether she lives close, and keep things light-hearted. You can start to get a little friendlier and even flirtatious once you've settled on a topic, but be cautious not to reveal too much of your intentions too soon when there's already a lot of skin on display.

In fact, the sea is where you have the highest opportunity to approach women at the beach. You can run around in the surf, body surf some waves, and overall just have fun next to some chicks. You can ask them to play a game, if you have a ball in the water, with them as a group and find out about their plans for the remainder of the day, how their day has gone, etc.

As a group, once you've earned their trust, you may start to get to know the person you like better and take the conversation to the next level while the others step aside to chat. Make plans to hang out later that evening or the following day, or suggest that you go out to dinner straight away to spend some additional time with her. Just keep in mind that she might not be prepared to part with her pals right away, so if necessary, suggest that they come join your group instead and proceed accordingly.

Chapter 9: Working

By at work, here I mean in the sense that a woman is working who you find attractive and would like to approach. This work environment could be any place where you find yourself receiving service from the woman of your dreams, such as a restaurant, bar, coffee shop, or store. The strategy itself isn't hard in this case because there's a clear reason you should speak with her—namely, so she can perform her duties. The tricky aspect is figuring out how to use this strategy to position yourself to ask her out on a date or for her number.

Either say, "Let's catch up time; what's your number?" or, if you have a pen handy, leave your own. This is a simple approach that relies only on your underlying charisma and the possibility that she will find your grin attractive enough to want to see you again.

Unless you're really attractive, this is usually not going to work. Instead, make the most of the brief time you have together by complimenting her, making a joke about someone in the store, or sharing a story about something related to her job that shows you two have things in common.

You should try to end this little two-minute conversation by mentioning how great she is and that you'd like to get to know her a little more because you'll be running out of time before she gets uncomfortable because she should be working. When you two get along well enough, she'll agree and give you her phone number.

Chapter Three: Boosting Your Confidence When Approaching Women

"Change your intention if you want to get rid of your fear of approaching women."

The majority of males are too shy to approach attractive women.

Which if you do what I'm about to share with you, it offers you a huge opportunity.

Many women lament that they are seldom contacted at all as it is not a woman's place to approach and make an attempt to pick up a man.

When guys approach them, it's usually to ask for their phone number, find out if they have a boyfriend, or offer to buy them a drink. Sometimes, they even tell them they want to take them out.

Why?

They have no notion of how to approach a woman in a proper manner.

Guys will also call her out on the street and gaze at her as she walks by. Additionally, the majority of males just stand or sit and stare at her when she's in public.

They lack the courage to approach her and hold a meaningful discussion with her.

You, therefore, have a very big opportunity.

You'll be the guy with his pick of ladies if you can be the kind of man who has the self-assurance to approach attractive women and make a good first impression.

You'll find there's absolutely no competition, which shocks a lot of males as well as startled me when I started pursuing women.

The majority of males merely observe and admire women. They only do that.

You will be able to choose from a wide selection of women after you possess the self-assurance to approach them appropriately.

Once you have the requisite skill sets and confidence, it's fairly easy.

How, then, can you develop that level of confidence?

Identifying what it means to be confident is the first step.

If you don't understand what confidence really is, it's quite simple to be confused about how you're feeling and why you're so frightened.

Let's define confidence now.

"Confidence (noun): belief in oneself and one's powers or abilities; self-confidence, self-reliance, assurance," according to the dictionary

The definition of the opposite term is another definition that will help you comprehend confidence completely.

And insecurities are that.

The dictionary definition of insecurity is self-doubt or a lack of confidence or assurance.

Put another way, insecurity results from a lack of confidence.

That's precisely how it operates.

You either exude confidence or insecurity.

So, how can you make that different?

It's easy. You must apply your intellect.

Your mind is a very strong instrument. You can choose to use your mental strength for good or evil.

Your poor self-perception will cause you to think in a way that feeds your fears.

Similarly, if you use your mind's power for good and for yourself, you'll think in a way that boosts your confidence.

Having said that, the following three suggestions are meant for beginners who want to learn how to use their mind's power and develop the courage to approach ladies.

Make it a habit to imagine successful outcomes.

Make it a practice to actually see the exchange between you and a woman you find attractive when you want to approach her.

In actuality, you don't even need to approach her. It's crucial to build up your bravery before making an approach.

Even after you've just pictured yourself approaching women, you might not feel safe doing so if you don't feel particularly secure around them.

But develop the habit of visualizing things going smoothly.

Instead of enabling insecure thoughts to overwhelm you, such as "What if I'm rejected?" "I'm probably going to run out of things to say," "What if she has a boyfriend?" "What will other people say when they see me approaching her?"

Instead of allowing those notions to take over your thinking, try to visualize the best-case situation.

Imagine walking up to her, making her smile, and starting a discussion. The start of the conversation is promising. The manner in which you communicate is one of the many reasons she finds you attractive.

Everything proceeded quite smoothly; she provided you with her phone number, and you left.

Later on, you get in touch with her to ask her out.

Though it doesn't totally address all of your confidence concerns with women, envisioning a successful outcome at least provides you a good start.

When you think about it, confidence is simply believing in your own abilities and self-worth.

You have to learn to believe in your own abilities rather than thinking that you are incapable or that things won't work out.

Believing in your ability to accomplish something instead of thinking you can't is the cornerstone of confidence when it comes to women.

By doing this, you're cultivating the habit of approaching women with optimism and confidence as opposed to negativity, anxiety, and self-doubt.

Which gets me to my next point.

Assess Yourself Thoroughly

The words that come from your lips are not as essential as how you carry yourself daily.

Look at yourself closely, the complete person. You don't have to drive a fancy automobile and wear pricey clothing to go about it. It has to do with appearance, self-assurance, self-worth, and self-care.

Personal cleanliness

It looks so easy. Basic hygiene. Don't we all do that? Surely we are not Stone Age barbarians?

You would be shocked at what some men think is presentable and at those who think women will react to their untidy, messy, and frequently foul-smelling exteriors.

Take frequent showers. Although it seems unnecessary to me, I must express it. And wash EVERYWHERE.

Make sure your nails are clean and trimmed. Consider getting a manicure. It is not in any way feminine. Women will notice, and they will react favorably.

Use mouthwash, floss, and brush your teeth. You wouldn't think I would have to say this again. a minimum of times daily. Along with carrying some gum, take caution while using mouthwash or breath sprays with strong medicinal scents.

Shave in the manner that suits you best. It's fantastic that you have a worn appearance, but even a scruffy look needs upkeep. To make her want to touch and kiss you, shave, trim, and apply cream to keep your scruff or beard smooth.

Pull those hairs out. Nostrils, ears, and back. Ask your barber or consider getting a wax job if you cannot reach them. There may be some pain, but it will be worthwhile.

Apply deodorant. Whatever celebrities may say about ditching the deodorant, don't follow their advice. Additionally, avoid using a body spray with a strong scent as a deodorant.

Be wary of cologne. Although you might think it helps you smell manly, the girl you're chatting to might interpret it as a warning sign or perhaps find the smell offensive. Thus, utilize it with caution. Ask some of your plutonic female friends what they think about it.

Observe good skin care. Maintain it hydrated and clean.

Cleanse your visage. Wash your face frequently and utilize medicine to treat breakouts if you are younger and have acne. Not only do young males experience it, I still occasionally get pimples and have to chuckle about it. Try using adult-specific care lotions to treat those unpleasant breakouts.

Observe good lip hygiene. A lady won't want to kiss a man with cracked and chapped lips. Always wear lip balm, and drink plenty of water.

Smoking. It's a personal decision if you smoke, but be aware that it poses health risks and discolors your teeth or fingers in addition to smelling bad. Every day, smoking rates are declining, and the likelihood of you continuing to smoke is high. Think about parting with it.

Don't wear sunglasses. When you speak, women want to look into your eyes and see what's in them. They object to seeing images of themselves.

The Way You Hold Yourself

Take a position facing a mirror. Take a deep breath and stand calm.

What do you look like?

Are you a slouch? Do you have a tall stance? Back shoulders? Do you fold your arms across your chest without thinking?

Your self-presentation and body language can have a big impact.

Everything will vary depending on who you ask. Everybody has physical strengths and weaknesses, some of which are changeable and others not. Recognize the physical attributes that work for you and those you want to improve.

Eye contact. Avoid staring, but do look into her eyes. There is a thin line.

Turn to face the person you are speaking with at all times.

Avoid fidgeting. When standing, equally distribute your weight across both feet.

Don't slouch; instead, stand up straight. It can give the impression that you're weaker or less manly. And bring their shoulders back.

If she approaches you, don't back down. It conveys a message of indifference, insecurity, or worse, timidity.

Avoid tensing your jaw. Unwind. It's also a known fact that women interpret slight lip-paring throughout a conversation as an attraction.

Listen to her with your head tilted. It demonstrates that you are paying attention to what they are saying.

Grin. a genuine grin. It ought to be manageable. Don't hold back when you hear something kind, humorous, or endearing.

Chapter 2: Where exactly do you go wrong in relationships?

"Do I just accept that I'm a flawed girl?"

"I get into relationships all the time; what could be going on?"

I still recall asking myself these questions after I ended my five-year relationship. I wanted nothing more in life than to flee from everyone and scream uncontrollably.

I acknowledge that my persona is nuanced. I also nag. I also tend to tell men how to treat me. (You are well aware that spoiling a lady is quite difficult.) Yes, indeed! Spoiling men is fairly easy. Because guys are so simple to please, it was incredibly difficult to comprehend why I couldn't retain them.

However, the most insightful discovery became clear after a thorough internal assessment. I narrowed my issues down to just three. Just three, can you imagine? And for more than five years, they cost me wholesome relationships.

I was playing too hard to get, falling in love with terrible dudes, and prioritizing high upkeep over high value.

These were difficult lessons, and I wouldn't wish them on you. I'll try to explain how you should stay away from this.

You keep falling in love with bad boys for this reason (and how to avoid it)

Have you ever asked God questions about relationships? Yes, I have. Not just once but multiple times. Some ladies are fortunate from birth. Once, of course, they fall in love—with a great guy. As a result, they tie the knot and begin living the life of a dominant pair.

The devil has then infiltrated the lives of most of us. We experience repeated heartbreaks, yet with each setback, we find ourselves entangled in the web of a wicked lad. Isn't life sometimes unfair?

Interestingly, even when it's abundantly clear that the bad male will never change, most women choose to stay with him.

I have seen bright, clever women mired in this situation for months, even years. This is before they can go.

However, why do ladies enjoy nasty boys?

Why are the bad lads so alluring that they keep us imprisoned for a long time?

If you have just been attracted to jerks all your life, let me make it plain that there is nothing wrong with you. All kinds of men are drawn to beautiful women: douchebags, narcissists, manipulators, great guys, and losers of all stripes. After all, moths and butterflies are drawn to even a scorching flame.

A study by DR. Breuning claims that most women are driven by powerful primitive instincts that lead them to think that terrible lads can defend them more effectively than "nice" guys. They also frequently think that for them to live long, healthy lives, they need a guy to take care of them and the kids.

According to research, 35% of women in relationships have ever been the victim of sexual abuse. The numbers may be higher because some women find it impolite to disclose instances of unhealthy partnerships. Is it, though?

You keep falling for bad boys, so blame your instincts. They are the reason your body, even in the face of abuse, disdain, and harsh treatment, persuades your naive soul that these individuals are superior to the excellent but lesser males out there.

It's interesting to note that terrible boys frequently exude extreme confidence, which satisfies your instincts and makes you think he's the one. These men have excellent bed manners as well. Their sexual act is incredibly hot since they are so self-assured. And it's tough for some ladies to leave such a handsome guy.

This group also includes narcissists. These guys have mastered keeping their actual selves hidden from their partners at the beginning of a relationship until they are certain they have set her off and trapped her. A narcissist's tendency to sing and dance about his broken past draws "nice girls" to him in an attempt to ease his excruciating agony. Before you realize it, you've fallen victim to a terrible love trap.

Additionally, narcissists enjoy telling us exactly what we want to hear. These are the kind of folks who will tell you straight-faced claims, half-truths and lies nonstop.

I mean, it's hard to stay away from the evil guys. It's not easy to change your natural inclinations, either. You can control your instincts by establishing clear boundaries that exclude anyone who behaves badly toward you. Follow your instincts and immediately end the relationship if you see any warning signs.

Dating a bad boy is often a dramatic experience. There comes a time when the drama becomes ingrained in your life, and you become addicted. Unfortunately, all of this turmoil eats up time and energy, which throws off our goals and plans. If you must get past this, remember that love differs from drama and suffering. In a relationship, drama, and suffering indicate a problem. Get out of that problematic relationship if you cannot resolve the issue.

I also learned a valuable lesson from my dating experience: never commit to anything until I'm positive about it. In the initial months of their friendship, bad guys, narcissists, and psychopaths are frequently very naive about commitment, but they quickly stop taking the connection seriously. Thus, think twice before calling him "the one"!

www.ingramcontent.com/pod-product-compliance
Lightning Source LLC
Chambersburg PA
CBHW052157110526
44591CB00012B/1985